David Bellamy's
PEMBROKESHIRE

HALSGROVE

First published in Great Britain in 2004

British Library Cataloguing-in-Publication Data
A CIP record for this title is available from the British Library

ISBN 1 84114 353 7

HALSGROVE
Halsgrove House
Lower Moor Way
Tiverton, Devon EX16 6SS
Tel: 01884 243242
Fax: 01884 243325
email: sales@halsgrove.com
website: www.halsgrove.com

Printed and bound by D'Auria Industrie Grafiche Spa, Italy

Contents

St Govan's Chapel   240 x 200mm

Dedication
To Jenny, Jo, Carrie and Catherine who have always made my time in
Pembrokeshire so enjoyable and so full of beautiful, crazy memories.

Foreword by Jenny Keal

Most of us have a strong attachment to our home county. The place where we were born and brought up will always have a special place in our heart, but when that county is one with a magnificent coastline, rich and fertile rolling farmland, an enchanting history and a sense of being 'at the end of the world' as Pembrokeshire does, it is no wonder that it becomes a major inspiration for an artist whose home it will always be, no matter where he lives.

David was truly blessed when he was born into a warm and loving family, and was brought up to appreciate the beauty of his rural surroundings. It is no surprise to me, having visited the places where he played and listened to his tales, that he has such strong feelings about the countryside and wild places. But this alone does not make an artist. David's passion for the outdoors created and developed his painting and that passion continues to nurture his gift every day.

This book allows us to share with him a little of that enthusiasm. He gives us a glimpse of his Pembrokeshire, where time stands still, the place that is his home.

Linney Head (above)
A roughly-handled sketch using water-colour pencils smudged with rain water to effect a crude rendering of the scene. These pencils allow me to create an image in all weathers.

Introduction

Strange though it may seem, despite being born in the shadow of the great keep of Pembroke Castle, it was only after leaving Pembrokeshire as an adult that I realised what truly beautiful scenery falls within the county. This westernmost county of Wales, sometimes called *Gwlad hud a lledrith*, or the land of magic and enchantment, is one of the most paintable in the country, and has attracted a great many artists over the centuries, including that great master, J.M.W. Turner. How others have viewed a place is always fascinating, whether in painting or description. The artist-author James Baker published *A Picturesque Guide to Wales* in the late eighteenth century and his comments on Narberth, my home-town, were interesting if stylistically predictable: 'There are two or three decent inns for refreshment, some shops of trade, and there is a tolerable market for provisions; but very few inhabitants of fashion in all the neighbourhood.' But things have moved on since then.

Many visitors think of Pembrokeshire purely in terms of its coastline, when in fact there are four distinctly different types of landform in the county. Apart from the outstanding coast, the upland areas of the Preseli Range, Treffgarne Mountain and the hills to the very north of the county with their craggy caps, while to the south the Daugleddau estuary with its many wooded creeks reveals a more intimate, almost secret landscape. All these are held together by the large mass of undulating pastoral countryside that itself holds so many scenic gems. This diversity of scenery is one of the main reasons why so many landscape artists have settled in the county.

Achieving a sense of place is for me a vital ingredient in a painting: it must have something of the soul of the place in order to have meaning. This involves observing the subtleties such as roofs and chimneys of traditional cottages, the style of farm gates, the wind-sculpted trees so common in Pembrokeshire, and much more. This sense of place touches on one's feelings – not unique to artists, but a powerful tool in creating that surge of inspiration that takes a painting from the ordinary to something more elevated.

For me these sensations occur not just when I am painting, but at times when I am far away, for example, when stuck down some crevass in an Alpine glacier and my thoughts turn longingly to Newgale Sands where one can feel so free with the smell of the salty surf on the Atlantic breeze, or perhaps to riding my little red childhood bike down the summer lane to Llanfallteg.

Nolton Haven

Heavy seas crash over the rock barrier on the north side of the haven. A water-soluble graphite pencil is really effective for such immediate, moody effects. I have on occasion combined it with sea water applied with a finger.

Cottage below Maiden Castle

It is not simply the visual response to a scene that matters. I find myself greatly moved by the threads of history, by legends and the feeling of belonging, all of which exude a compelling presence in Pembrokeshire. When sketching a humble cottage I wonder who lived there, and what sort of life they lived. While I have sketched wrecks on the county's coastline, as I draw rocks and cliffs my mind often strays to what it must be like to find your vessel being smashed up on these shores when a storm is raging. So much of the Preseli uplands invoke feelings of being close to the ancient people whose stones symbolise more than just the bones of raw landscape, and who scraped a life on these hills long before the Romans invaded these shores. Such feelings manifest themselves in the stories that accompany my descriptions and paintings, for they are intricately bound into my inspirational senses.

In the main I rarely paint finished watercolours out of doors, preferring to carry out sketches, sometimes in colour, and generally backing them up with photographs and notes. Sometimes the best sketches are those where the elements take a hand in the work – perhaps where rain has spattered the watercolour into confused patterns and blobs, where the wind has blown a page into the mud, or the mess resulting from closing the sketchbook prematurely whilst washes are still wet. Back in the studio I turn these scenes into paintings, often changing the elements, especially the sky and the mood, to suit the composition. Many subjects I repeat over the years, in different seasons, times of day and circumstance, losing track of how many times I've painted the Cleddau, Angle, Fishguard, and other favourites.

The coastline can present harsh demands on those who wish to explore its every nook and cranny. Early on when I stuck mainly to the coastal path, I realised there were many impressive subjects lying beneath the cliffs, and that the best place for sketching was rarely the cliff-top. Enticing caves, natural arches, pinnacles, coves, and a multitude of fascinating natural features beckoned, but were tantalisingly out of reach unless more drastic methods were employed. Boats resolved some of these problems, especially around St David's, Solva, Fishguard and Tenby, allowing me to get in close to these fascinating subjects. My painting courses in north Pembrokeshire have often included a sketching trip on a boat. At sea level the awkward acute angles caused by looking down on a subject were gone, so perspective became easier, and at the same time the low viewpoint accentuated drama. Additionally the wildlife became more evident, being so much closer.

It was a short step to trying out a kayak. This had the advantage of allowing me to land ashore on remote coves to work on the rocks and beaches, and in sea-caves. Sketching from a bobbing kayak however, even when reasonably calm is not easy, although it helps to have a second kayak alongside holding on to your own. I remember sketching in the cavern at St Non's Bay when every wave that surged in lifted the kayak high up, rasping me up against the side of the cave, a rise and fall of several feet which of course made a challenging sketching scenario!

Eventually, I turned to the belly-boat as a more stable platform, though still using a variety of craft to meet different objectives. Belly-boats are basically large inner tubes from trucks, covered with a tough cordura shell in which there are pockets for equipment. A comfortable back-rest formed by two independent inflatable bags allows one to recline as though in an inflatable armchair, while sitting on a cross-piece. They are

Cottages near St Davids   200 x 300mm
Against a dark, angry sky the light-coloured grouted roofs of these old cottages stand out like beacons. While there are still many remaining, these traditional roofs are sadly being replaced by soulless modern materials.

David Balbany

used by anglers on placid lakes and not really designed for rough water or at sea. I first used it at sea at Lydstep, choosing a day of lowering sky so that I would be unlikely to be seen and potentially 'rescued' against my will. Having inflated the craft I strode out of my cave in wetsuit and flippers, carrying the inflatable. Unfortunately a couple stood watching from along the beach as I staggered towards the water – not having worn flippers before, I found they kept throwing up large chunks of sand and causing me to lurch across the beach in a somewhat drunken manner.

Quickly I reverted to walking backwards into the water, aware that the couple up the beach were studying every move with interest. Once in deeper water I tried to insert my leg into the bottom of the belly-boat, but as I stood poised on one leg, the other seeking the entry point, a large wave hit me broadside on and I went flying. So I retreated to some round rocks, sat down, and with difficulty managed to get into the craft. I then carried out what can only be described as a backward waddle into deeper water, waving to the beach as I went. Thankfully I soon reached deep water and then enjoyed a whole minute of floating about before a wave deposited me onto a flat rock. It took some time to extricate myself off this perch and then carry on into the next cove where I did some sketching. Despite this rather woeful start the belly-boat has proved amazingly useful in getting into some impressive locations.

Sketching in the belly-boat.

Previous pages: **Green Bridge of Wales and Stack Rocks** *520 x 700mm*
The spectacular cliff architecture is seen to great advantage from this viewpoint, the reverse of most pictures of the Green Bridge. The miniscule birds suggest a sense of scale.

Little Haven   210 x 230mm

Carew Castle   170 x 200mm

Carew Castle has been a favourite subject of artists down the years, including Paul Sandby, Sir Richard Colt Hoare, J.M.W. Turner and Henry Gastineau. In the fifteenth century it was home to the colourful Sir Rhys ap Thomas, who vowed to Richard III that an enemy would land in Wales only over his dead body. When Henry Tudor landed at Dale, Rhys hid under Mullock Bridge as Henry marched over it, to ease his sense of guilt. He was knighted on the battlefield of Bosworth when Richard was defeated with the help of a large Welsh army.

Preseli Slopes   180 x 320mm

Traversing on foot from bays and coves under the cliffs, sometimes in shorts and sandals, sometimes in wetsuit, has been another useful method of locating stunning scenery. Although at times it involved an incredible effort with a combination of rock gymnastics, swimming, wading and jumping, it might yield absolutely nothing by way of pictorial material, but always provided an immensely satisfying trip. Naturally it was critical to be aware of the state of the tide and sea conditions before setting out. Protecting sketching equipment and camera was also a prime consideration, and these are contained within waterproof bags and boxes.

Pembrokeshire is a land of contrasts, and has something for everyone, whether artist or not. Most of it is cultivated, and while I love painting these places, it is in that part of the county '…with all the horrid graces of the wilderness itself,' as Lord Shaftesbury wrote in 1709, that my heart soars. The majority of the coastline remains untamed, and inland there are pockets of wildness that provide a breathing-space for those who feel hemmed in and stressed by the over-civilised twenty-first-century. This wildness is vital for the sanity of many, to allow them to recharge their batteries, to touch the real earth once again, as we did so much when I roamed these pastures as a child. The countryside is now under considerable threat from many forms of development, so I feel it is important to understand the need not just for natural beauty, but for craggy landscape, untamed moorland, natural woodland or simply just a briar entanglement, untainted by man's interference. Indeed, many individual natural features such as rocks, trees and caves become so familiar that they are like old friends, steadfast and always there when I return.

Beddarthur
A location with possible connections with King Arthur. Beddarthur translates as 'the grave of Arthur.'

Left: *Negotiating a steep traverse*

This book describes those parts of Pembrokeshire that matter most to me, especially those where I keep returning to paint and sketch. Nevertheless, much fascinating scenery and locations have been omitted because of lack of space, for it would take several books to cover it all. Some of the scenery will be familiar to many, some will be new, and there are several views of well-known scenes painted from an unfamiliar angle. At times it can be quite a trial to come up with new views: painting the same views as everyone else has little appeal.

Leaving Pembrokeshire in 1961 made me long for it even more: this overpowering sense of *hiraeth* – the longing – is part of every Welsh person who moves away. Simply going on holiday does not generate

that intense feeling of loss when you have been away from the old country for so long. Sketching and painting in the Himalayas, the Peruvian Andes, the Serengeti Plain, the deserts of Arabia, and so much more, has presented me with spectacular scenery, but the most heartfelt privilege is always to return like salmon after their long wanderings, to my scenes of childhood. Whilst it is not peculiar to the Welsh, this strong sense of belonging seems to be missing in many cultures.

Pembrokeshire to me is more than just a place to paint its glorious scenery or explore its lovely countryside: it tugs deep inside at the very heart-strings.

2

Running with the tide

Soaring cliffs of wildly-shattered limestone, towering stacks, rock arches, sea caverns and blowholes make the south coast of Pembrokeshire one of the most dramatic of landscape forms in the country.

Erosion of the limestone over the millennia has formed a remarkable array of natural features which look as though they have been subjected to the attention of a giant sledge-hammer, wielded by someone with an aesthetic appreciation of natural forms, as the shapes are so replete with distorted delight. For the walker, landscape artist, photographer,

naturalist or geologist this is a truly outstanding area of stunning scenery, brought to life by the constant swell of the sea and the cries and swoops of swarming seabirds.

The Pembrokeshire Coast National Trail begins at Amroth, a pleasant coastal village with an immense expanse of beach at low tide. Between Wiseman's Bridge and Saundersfoot, great ribs of the coal measures jut out of the beach, interspersed with beautiful rock pools backed by the huge red crag of Coppet Hall Point. When viewed from the beach the rocks form a powerful focal point for artist or photographer, but

Amroth   130 x 330mm

from the coast path, the great semicircular pattern of these ribs becomes more evident.

Here the coast path mainly follows the old Saundersfoot Railway Company line, taking in three tunnels beneath some rather unstable-looking cliffs. The railway originally ran from Saundersfoot Harbour to Stepaside Iron Works, turning inland before reaching Wiseman's Bridge, to climb up Pleasant Valley. Initially, horse-drawn trams carried the coal and iron, until locomotive power took over early in the twentieth century.

At Monkstone Point, Tenby comes into view. During the Middle Ages, Tenby was a busy port, second in importance only to Bristol in the Channel, and trading not just locally but with Spain, Portugal and France. By the end of the nineteenth century, the harbour was crammed with fishing smacks.

The artist is well served in Tenby: in summer the old harbour usually contains many boats worth painting, with a picturesque backdrop of tall Regency houses, many of colour-washed stucco, the spire of St Mary's church, and other attractive buildings. Across the water from Castle Beach the Victorian St Catherine's Fort looks down from its own craggy island, the rock gouged into caves in places.

The Tudor Merchant's House, owned by the National Trust, is one of the town's finest architectural gems, making a fine sketching subject when sunlight falls across it. Next door stands the former home of the Victorian artist Charles Norris, a great character for keeping the local authorities in order. In the considerable collection of his artwork, Tenby has a fine record of much of the town and neighbourhood before the advent of photography.

Tenby of course was the birthplace of Augustus John, who studied under Edward J. Head before going on to the Slade in 1894. His sister Gwen followed a year later. During the summer of 1897 he hit his head on a rock while diving into the sea off Giltar Point, and was said to have emerged from the water as a Bohemian genius. Certainly by the 1920s he was the leading portrait painter in the country. By comparison, Gwen

Corner of Tenby Harbour

did not share her brother's flamboyant style. She eventually settled in Paris as mistress to Auguste Rodin. Gwen only painted one landscape of Tenby, preferring figures, interiors and cats as subjects.

I loved our early family visits to Tenby, especially when my cousins joined us on the beach, although they were generally tame days compared with the adventures I've put Catherine, my daughter, through, especially in the early days at Lydstep.

Dylan Thomas's Boathouse   160 x 330mm
Although just outside the Pembrokeshire border, Laugharne is close to where I was brought up, and is crammed with attractive subjects which excite the artist, including a castle, muddy creeks and mud-caked boats, many of which will never go to sea again.

Overleaf: **Tenby Harbour   240 x 551mm**

David Bellamy

The author sketching at Tenby with an A5 sketchbook for rapid work.

Tenby from Caldey Island   230 x 420mm

On a clear day Foelcwmcerwyn is visible rising above Tenby when seen from Caldey. The interplay of shadows and light on the buildings created exciting nuances, and I simply waited for the light to fall on the part I was most interested in accentuating.

Smugglers' Cave, Lydstep   210 x 170mm

South-west of Tenby lies the spectacular stretch of coastline at Lydstep Head. In the days of sailing ships sloops would load limestone at Lydstep Bay to carry across to North Devon and other destinations, but now in summer it is the playground of noisy jet-skis and fast boats. The shattered limestone cliffs of the headland reveal impressive vertical bedding. In places one wonders how the rock structures actually stay up and don't come crashing down at the slightest movement of the sea. This is a popular area with climbers, especially Mother Carey's Kitchen, a sheer cliff with gaping gashes at the bottom which suggest a suitable site for a witches' coven.

The walk around Lydstep Head holds dramatic interest all the way, a veritable limestone switchback with sensational drops to sea level. Caldey and St Margaret's Islands can be seen just offshore, and to the east, Worm's Head and the Gower peninsula are visible on a reasonably clear day.

Catherine recalls how one December when she was about four years old, we visited Caverns Beach, I left her on the beach then waded round a cliff in boots and rucksack to sketch an arch. After about twenty minutes or so she began to wonder if I was OK, when I suddenly appeared round the corner, '...in it up to his chin and dripping with seaweed!' By then she was pretty used to strange episodes in pursuit of pictures, and we have had much fun traversing these cliffs.

West of Caverns Beach the coast path skirts Skomar Tower, with a subsidiary path leading to the airy summit of the tower itself, not for those of a nervous disposition. The view back down towards Caverns Beach will hold you in awe, especially on a day of wild seas, the huge natural arch forming a striking focal point. Only the lowest of spring tides allow easy access. There are a number of caverns here, some used by smugglers in days gone by, and it takes little imagination to dream up sea monsters in a place like this.

From Skomar Tower the path runs along the top of the cliffs to Skrinkle Haven, which is on the fault line of carboniferous limestone and Old Red Sandstone, a dramatic transition. Skrinkle, formerly part of the Manorbier army range, has been made accessible via a great many steps, but it is worth the effort of descending to Church Doors, particularly at low tide. A narrow through cave, easily missed, in the high right-hand

Lydstep Pinnacle
A watercolour sketch more finished than usual. In the days of sailing vessels, sloops would load up with limestone on this beach for export.

Caverns Beach, Lydstep   210 x 450mm
This view can only be seen at very low spring tides, which give access to spectacular limestone cliff scenery of caves, arches and soaring buttresses.

Natural bridge, Skomar Tower

rocky rampart leads from the smaller cove with its tall natural arch, to the large attractive beach beyond.

If you do go through this route keep an eye on the tide, as it is easy to become cut off, although once while sketching, my need to capture the subject was more important than getting wet, so we had an interesting traversing scramble to return via the cave. Jenny my wife and her two daughters, Joanne and Caroline, were with me, as well as Catherine, but not one agreed that 'it was good character-building stuff' – they'd already done all that! Caroline needs much cajoling to join us on a walk, but if there is a hint of danger involved she is often first to go. She has been known to insist that we climb all unnecessary routes up crags on the beach over 60 feet high, even when we can easily walk round them.

St Govan's Head is only accessible when the Castlemartin army range is not firing, so this area can only be entered when the red flags are not flying. Enormous boulders litter the foreshore beneath the cliffs, providing a graphic example of coastal erosion. The cliffs are often festooned with climbers who abseil down to the wave-cut platform and then climb back up. From the headland, Stackpole Head and Church Rock to the east are often brought graphically to life in late afternoon sunlight.

Further west, just below a car park, the tiny St Govan's Chapel is wedged into the cliffs and reached by steep steps. The chapel, in its setting of wild cliffs, is a must for artists, with a particularly fine aspect from the water's edge. St Govan himself is thought to have been a sixth century Irish hermit, though other theories link him to Sir Gawain of Arthurian fame.

The chapel apparently once had a silver bell with which Govan would warn seafarers of the perils of the rocky coastline. This did not go down too well with the local wreckers, so they sent a deputation of suitably-armed villains to sort old Govan out. As the ill-doers approached, Govan prayed to God and squeezed against a rock, which promptly wrapped itself round him. The gang could not find him, but stole the bell. Govan emerged from his hideaway leaving an impression in the rock which can be seen today. As the pirates made their getaway a storm blew up and sank their boat. The bell was rescued by sea-nymphs, placed near the chapel and entombed within a rock. It is said that the rock rings out when struck.

Manorbier Castle   190 x 330mm

This magnificent Norman stronghold is viewed here from the sea. It had a fairly peaceful history: nobody seemed to want to attack it, probably because it defended no main routes or town. Giraldus Cambrensis, son of Gerald of Windsor and the lovely Nesta, was born in the castle in 1147 and is best known for his Itinerary through Wales, *a journey he made with Archbishop Baldwin in 1188 with the aim of recruiting for the Third Crusade.*

Freshwater East   180 x 280mm

After centuries of battering – a sustained and salt-edged violence –
waves have smashed crude doorways through
where the wrecked cliff stands with jutting walls now gaping,
beleaguered and defiant still, but shaking
as the bullish ocean roars.

Jean M. Harvey

Opposite: ***Crags in Barafundle Bay   220 x 320mm***

David Bellamy

Broad Haven panorama   110 x 470mm   *Viewed from St Govan's Head with Church Rock rising Excalibur-like in the middle of the bay.*

Saddle Bay

Overleaf: **Sunlight and mist, St Govan's   360 x 670mm**
Seen from the very tip of St Govan's Head, it is possible to make out the
chapel jammed in the cliffs, but it needs extreme care to get this view.

David Bellamy

Exploring at sea level, Caroline leading.

Continuing westwards we pass a number of headlands with sunken areas and holes in the ground in places. In many of these blowholes you can hear surf crashing below, usually accompanied by pressure waves. They are highly-dangerous places and not the place for casual exploration. A little way along is the site of Ogof Govan, a cave naturally decorated with outstanding formations. The main entrance is half-way down a cliff.

One December afternoon under a grey sky matched by grey rock and a grey sea, several grey, tense faces gazed down the cliff in search of the entrance, which is not visible from above. One by one we roped down. The recommended mode of entry is by abseiling down to a point level with the entrance, then swinging in, either grabbing a rock as you do so, or relying on a friend to grab you before you swing out again above the waves. Brent Durban, who is always obliging in such matters, actually swung in several times so that I could obtain a suitable rendering on paper: sketching a swinging figure can be somewhat demanding.

Inside the cave a roomy crawling passage leads to a slot, and once through light can be seen ahead. This comes from a rock window in the cliff, a grand balcony from which to view the waves crashing in below. A 90-degree turn then leads to a nasty little hole through which one has to squeeze. I became jammed and could not move either forwards or backwards, my breathing sounding like a turkey in a barrel-full of hyenas. I decided to simply rest and let my body completely relax. After a couple of minutes my breathing became more controlled. I then managed to thrust myself through, scraping my chest and fervently hoping to be able to reverse the process when it became time to leave.

Gratefully I slumped into the welcoming comfort of a muddy pool. Some of the lads were having more difficulty than myself and Brent calmly proceeded to offer a remarkable series of suggested movements for propelling a human body through an orifice several sizes too small. This went on for some time, but three of the lads had to abandon the attempt. Further crawling passage led to a magnificent chamber with countless beautiful formations reflected in a clear blue-green, lagoon-like pool. A massive column stood in the middle flanked by two large varicoloured stalagmites. Suddenly coming upon such glorious natural treasures was both humbling and mind-blowing. I stayed some time to sketch, eventually emerging into the intense blackness of the December night to climb back up the cliff.

West of Stack Rocks lies forbidden country, as Range West is only accessible on a National Park guided walk. Arguably it is not as interesting as the coastline further east, but it is a shame that in a national park this part is denied to the casual visitor, or those who do not wish to walk in a group. For much of the walk to Linney Head the eye is drawn to the prominent pinnacle of Pen yr Holt Stack as it gradually gets larger. From certain angles it is said to resemble General de Gaulle.

Some of the cliffs around Pen yr Holt Bay look as though they would collapse under the weight of my 3B pencil were I foolish enough to drop it. Fossils are common. Here and there acute folds in the rock strata contort into reptilian-like features, which in the gloom seem to come to life. As Linney Head approaches, the horizon is littered with burnt-out tanks, a sharp reminder not to go touching nasty metal things in the undergrowth.

Main Chamber, Ogof Gofan   200 x 290mm
This is one of the finest-decorated chambers in the country, the formations reflected in the blue-green lagoon in the centre. It is not an easy cave to reach. The figure giving scale is Dewi Durban.

At Linney Head the coastline turns north, with access to the coast once more restored at Freshwater West, an enormous expanse of beach wide open to the ravages of the Atlantic. The lack of high cliffs gives it a wonderful sense of spaciousness with big skies. One November afternoon, having driven for ages, I eagerly raced out with sketchbook into skitting rain and a fierce breeze. Sunlight at times burst through the swirling clouds as great breakers crashed onto the rocks. It created a wildness and dynamism that made me feel so alive. The rain did not matter, for I worked with watercolour pencils, and as so often happens, nature had a much more accomplished way of enhancing the sketch than my own awkward marks.

Freshwater West is a great place to sit and contemplate, and get away from the stresses of life. Behind the beach lie sand dunes, the sand blowing across the road in places. A small reed-thatched seaweed collector's hut stands above the beach, restored by the National Park authority. These huts were originally used to dry out seaweed in preparation for laver bread, and at one time many huts stood along this part of the coast.

From Freshwater West, the jagged coastline continues round to West Angle Bay. Just after 8 pm on the evening of Thursday, February 15, 1996, the 147,000-tonne tanker *Sea Empress* ran aground nearby, at the entrance to Milford Haven. During the next few days over 72,000 tonnes of crude oil were spilled into the sea as the salvage operation took place.

The government, with breathtaking arrogance, refused to call it a disaster and tried to play down the whole incident, yet it damaged more protected wildlife sites than any other pollution incident in Britain. The whole affair seemed like a black farce: it took nine days before the oil began to be pumped out of the vessel.

The Pembrokeshire coast is one of the most environmentally sensitive coastlines in the UK, yet the Whitehall authorities still seem to treat it in a cavalier manner. The visual impact of the spill has mainly disappeared, but who knows how long the environment will take to recover, or indeed when the next accident will happen?

Devil's Pathway, Flimston

Guillemots on Stack Rocks   145 x 210mm

In late spring, there is nowhere in Britain so easy to view a major seabird colony than Elegug Stacks. I once witnessed this amazing spectacle having just returned from the Greek Islands where I hardly saw a single bird, yet here the guillemots were crammed onto the stacks. Once the breeding season is under way, there is so little room that as one bird lands in an ungainly two-point crash, another is usually knocked off its perch. After about three weeks the chicks simply leap off the cliffs, never having flown before – what confidence!

Clearing Skies, Angle   _220 x 330mm_

Angle is one of my favourite sketching locations, a veritable feast of mud when the tide is out. Then I can wander around the bay in wellies, sketching the wealth of subject matter, whether boats, cottages, the lovely old church, Peel tower, glistening channels in the mud, or posts dripping with seaweed.

3

South of the Landsker

The Landsker – an imaginary line splitting the Welsh north of Pembrokeshire from the English south – is betrayed even today by the names of the villages: apart from a few places such as Llangwm the anglicised south reveals few truly Welsh names.

The original line followed a series of castles flung up to exclude the Welsh from the south: from Roch Castle in the west to Laugharne in the east. The old buildings of the south were more substantial, whether farm or church. Tall battlemented church towers could act as lookouts in case of

Pembroke Castle   170 x 255mm
The castle is seen here from the Pembroke River. In his paintings, Turner altered the foreground to suggest boisterous seas, often with a raging tempest for dramatic background to the castle.

Penbank
This was our home in Llanddewi for ten years. We used the anglicised form of spelling, which I've retained here.

attack by the neighbours from the north, whose buildings tended to be more humble.

I was brought up with one foot on either side of the Landsker, in the village of Llanddewi Velfrey. We lived high on a hill with marvellous views of the Preseli Hills, and though there was no running water or electricity, these were truly happy days. We fetched water from a well on Llanddewi Gaer, the old hillfort behind us where Malcolm, my brother, and I would play all day; a wonderful place for adventures.

Every year Llanddewi would hold a village eisteddfod, and although my singing was pretty abysmal, I always managed to win the painting compe-

tition. The down side was that I had to sit through a whole afternoon of singing before I could go up on the stage to claim my two shillings and sixpence (10.25p) prize.

Things were not easy in those post-war days. I loved reading and drawing, but had little by way of art materials, having to tear out the blank endpapers of books to obtain drawing paper. Even the backs of cereal packets had their uses. School powder paints did little to inspire me, but somehow I thrived on art and it was easily my best subject. But as a youngster, I never had any thoughts of becoming an artist, for in Pembrokeshire in those days people mainly went into teaching or farming.

Barn at Llanddewi Velfrey   210 x 300mm

Lane to Llanddewi Church
160 x 135mm

Between Caerau Gaer and Llanddewi Gaer, this lane is lined on one side with splendid beeches as it dips down into the lovely Vale of Marlais. The old village of Llanddewi Velfrey used to be situated near the church, but with the coming of the A40 the village gravitated northwards, leaving just a scattering of cottages and farms on the old site.

Approaching Henllan *160 x 200mm*

As a youngster I walked this lane many times, for it connected our house with that of my grandfather (his house is seen in the distance). Here I have included my father returning the horse and cart to Henllan Farm after fetching a load of horse-manure for the garden.

Dad cycled to work in Narberth as a carpenter every day. I loved going to visit him in his workshop, with its pleasant smells of sawn wood. He often stood knee-deep in wood-shavings with a broad welcoming grin across his face. He liked nothing better than to spend a day fishing, at the time a vital supplement to our food. We passed many happy hours beside the Taf and the Marlais rivers.

Sometimes most of the family would fish together into the night, and I remember Grandad in his eighties having difficulty landing a whopper in the dark. Eventually we found his line had been caught up a tree, and the wind convinced him that nothing less than a ten-pound salmon was on the end.

One time after a day's fishing with my friend Andrew, for some reason we took a different route home – I believe this was because a bull was involved – and we found ourselves on the wrong side of the Marlais. I wasn't too keen on a long detour, so took a flying leap across the river, hit the far bank and fell backwards into the water. That was probably instrumental in triggering my later penchant for constantly getting wet.

Bulls could be quite a problem, and I became adept at the rapid climbing of trees and penetrating a thick thorn hedge at speed. On Orielton Farm, between Llanddewi and Narberth, my uncle always maintained that the ground itself had some strange effect on the animals and induced wildness. Along this route Mam would walk to Narberth from Henllan House, and more than once she had to run for her life with a fearsome Welsh Black in pursuit. She could clear a five-bar gate without hesitation. Grandad, too had a life-threatening experience with the bull and was only saved when his retriever hung on to the bull's throat and distracted it while Grandad made good his escape.

Grandad had many adventures fighting with the Sherwood Rangers in the Boer War, often using his amazing trail-craft to warn officers of impending attacks, and having to sort out the resulting debacle when they ignored his advice. He later became a gamekeeper on the Henllan estate in Llanddewi. At times he would hide up trees waiting to ambush poachers. His sister Win was quite a shot with the gun, and there was much friendly rivalry between them. On one occasion he challenged her

Orielton Farm

A cross-country route runs between Henllan and Narberth past this farm, and in her younger days Mam was on occasion chased by a particularly nasty Welsh Black bull. She became rather adept at leaping over five-bar gates.

Opposite: **White Mill   230 x 185mm**
Many of our fishing trips on the River Marlais began here: sadly the river is no longer the superb trout stream it was in my schooldays.

to hit his backside from across the field, and duly bent over to bare his backside, which she promptly hit, fair and square!

Narberth to us was the big city. On a Thursday, Friday and Saturday, the WI hut was turned into a cinema, a highlight as we had no television in those days – I was ten years old before I saw my first television set. The four-mile walk home in the dark after the show did not bother us in the slightest, as we were so used to hiking across the countryside, night or day, whatever the weather. In snow we were often without buses as they could not get up Pengawse Hill to the east of Llanddewi.

Occasionally we would fish and explore the Eastern Cleddau, but it was not until later in life when I took up painting full-time that I grew to love the river. So often on a fine evening I would slip down from Mam's to Landshipping and sketch the tranquil scenery. Each time it was different: the state of the tide, a new boat, not to mention the atmosphere, weather and seasons. Rarely did I meet anyone. I have sketched the Cleddau more than any other subject, even more than my favourite mountains.

It is difficult to imagine now, but years ago much of Pembrokeshire was mined for coal. During the first half of the nineteenth century, mining for high-quality anthracite was a big industry around Landshipping, which today is a haven of peace and solitude. The coal was carried by barge to Lawrenny or Llangwm where it would be transferred on to larger vessels. At the Garden Pit near Landshipping Quay, the largest of the county's collieries, the workings ran under the River Daugleddau. Many of those who worked in the mines were women and children. Despite warnings that the coalface was perilously close to the river bed, and apparent signs of seepage, the miners were ordered to work as usual, their misgivings dismissed.

On February 14, 1844, as a high tide surged up the Daugleddau, the water broke through into the mine workings. Over forty men and boys were drowned, one boy as young as eleven years of age. That disaster, the worst in the history of the Pembrokeshire coalfield, more or less ended coal mining in the immediate area, although the Hook colliery on the western side of the Cleddau continued production until 1948.

Downstream from Landshipping many creeks, or pills, lead off from the main waterway as it journeys on to Milford Haven. At low tide these are muddy places, but even mud has a charm when glistening in the sunshine. The gnarled and twisted roots of trees which form into weird and contorted shapes exposed in the eroded banks of the river, inspired the abstracts of the painter Graham Sutherland. He spent many days at Benton Castle, sketching along the foreshore. At Lawrenny, one wide creek runs eastwards from the Daugleddau and again splits; one branch, the Cresswell River winds up to Cresswell Quay, the other to Carew with its splendid castle and tide mill. This is a secret, magical landscape, the light picking out new subjects for the artist as it drifts across woods and creeks.

To the south, Pembroke is dominated by the magnificent castle with its great keep. The castle, every boy's idea of what a real castle should look like, has been the subject of numerous artists down the centuries. There is a charming nineteenth-century watercolour of it by William Henry Bartlett, and an earlier one by Paul Sandby. J.M.W. Turner painted the castle several times, usually expanding the foreground to oceanic proportions. It can be painted effectively from several angles, including from the main street. When she was about five years old, Catherine came with me to sketch the castle from the pond, and while I emphasised the imposing building across the water, she drew in a tiny castle dwarfed by a line of gigantic ducks.

My early years were spent in the town of Pembroke Dock, where Mam lived during the war while Dad was away trying to shoot down the Luftwaffe. Unfortunately they seemed to have a real grievance against 'PD,' as the town was affectionately called locally, and Mam often related how she would be running through the streets with me while bombs were dropping all round.

One night in 1940 they scored a direct hit on the oil tanks, causing a fire which raged for eighteen days. The Pembrokeshire firemen were augmented by brigades from Carmarthen, Swansea, Cardiff, Newport, Bristol, Birmingham and other places. Five from the Cardiff brigade were killed when oil shot out of the tank and the resulting burst of flame engulfed them.

Narberth Castle   220 x 290mm
The castle featured prominently in the Mabiniogion, a collection of early tales. It is now quite ruinous.

Llawhaden Castle

One of the line of castles forming the Landsker, standing high above the Eastern Cleddau. In the Middle Ages, only the English incomers were allowed to trade in the settlement. In the thirteenth century, Bishop Beck founded a hospital here for paupers, pilgrims, elderly folk and imbeciles.

Opposite: **Blackpool Mill   260 x 240mm**

River Cleddau

The evening light spreads subtle tangerine,
the elbow of the river rests its arm,
cradles a soft swathe of silent trees
and mirrors back a deep, unruffled calm.

The boats are moored, at rest upon the mud,
the tide's receded to its lowest ebb
and sunset holds each mast in sharp relief,
its rigging etched and empty as a web

strung to catch the last few scraps of day,
as shadows deepen and the dark makes claim
to earth and air and water, dousing fire –
it slowly snuffs an April sky's last flame.

Jean M. Harvey

River Cleddau at Landshipping   210 x 315mm
This is the place I have painted more than any other. It has a special, haunting atmosphere, especially on a tranquil summer evening when the sounds of rustling reeds and lapping water are broken only by the cry of a curlew.

Strangely, my first and last cricket matches for Narberth Grammar School were both against Pembroke Dock Coronation School. I forget how I fared in the first game, but opening the batting in the final game I was still not out at the end when all the other ten batsmen had been dismissed – not that 18 is a great score for the time I was at the crease, although I do recall clouting a six into the main road immediately after being told to play defensively.

For the greater part of the nineteenth century, Pembroke Dock was the most advanced shipyard in the world, building the first steam-driven man o' war, the first warship fitted with a screw-propeller, and hundreds of naval vessels, including battleships. No less than five royal yachts were built there. Sadly, the Admiralty closed down the dockyard in 1926 because of its remoteness from the seat of government.

During the 1890s Milford began to be developed as a fishing port used by steam trawlers and fishing smacks. By the end of the First World War it was the fourth largest fishing UK port by value of fish landed, behind Hull, Grimsby and Fleetwood, the fleet comprising over 100 trawlers. After the Second World War a remorseless decline set in and gradually the fleet diminished. Many fishermen felt sold out by their own government when quotas were being negotiated. The fishing industry, like farming, has far too much ill-considered political interference, little of which seems to be in the interests of the fishermen and farmers of Wales.

Llangwm from Blacktar Point

Llangwm was once famous for its distinctive fisherwomen who were tough, fierce females who thought nothing of walking 30 miles with their baskets to Carmarthen to sell their fish, oysters, shrimps, cockles and mussels. Their baskets sometimes weighed a hundredweight or more. Although Llangwm is about 6 miles inland, I did once get cut off by the tide here and had to scramble across 150 yards of rocks to avoid getting wet.

Lawrenny   220 x 330mm

This is viewed from the nose of land between the tidal creeks of the Cresswell and Carew Rivers. The rocks here appear to have been designed for the artist, for not only are they most comfortable to sit on, but have handy grooves for retaining pencils, brushes and pens without them rolling into the undergrowth. During the Second World War this stretch of water was home to Walrus biplane flying-boats, which were used for reconnaissance and rescue duties.

River above Cresswell Quay

Opposite: **Cresswell Quay   250 x 330mm**
Without doubt the most tranquil spot in the world! The pub is highly popular on a sunny summer evening. The quay was once used to load coal from the nearby mines onto barges which were taken downstream to be transferred onto larger vessels.

David Bellamy

Most of the boats in the modern marina hold little interest to me artistically, but it is still possible to find a few working boats that excite the palette. During the Second World War flying-boats were based here, and the first aircraft I ever climbed into was a Short Sunderland flying-boat, not that I remember much about it.

My favourite spot in the haven is the eastern bay of Angle, which never fails to inspire. There is so much to paint: a variety of boats, cottages, an old ivy-clad tower, the church, and of course all that glorious mud at low tide. The stream oozes through the mud, with the occasionally weed-draped rib of an old wooden boat sticking up. There used to be a huge set of ribs lying in the harbour like the skeleton of a dinosaur, but time has now taken its toll. At low tide, muddy rivulets can be repositioned to lead in to picturesque fishing boats lying on their sides. Beyond the cottages stands the Old Point House, a pub formerly used by smugglers, without doubt a fine place to escape from the pressures of the rat race.

Brunt Farm

Opposite: **Loveston Church   250 x 221mm**
*Like many Pembrokeshire churches, this one featured a tall tower. The old milk churns
really appealed to me. Many is the time I had a lift on the milk lorry on my way to school,
and the cab always seemed so deliciously warm on a frosty winter's morning.*

Bridge near Reynaldton
210 x 160mm

Winter Fields, Yerbeston   170 x 320mm

4

Ups and Downs in St Bride's Bay

The Atlantic hits the west coast of Pembrokeshire with such a ferocity that in its wildest moments spume crashes over the tops of 200-foot/60m cliffs. With the sea roaring a fury and sound that seems to rattle the very foundations of the cliffs, it provides the artist with an ideal opportunity to render a sense of movement and atmosphere in a work.

Many a time have I lain prone on the cliffs, weighing down the sketch-book – and sometimes myself – with stones and rocks, while a storm rages and the sea froths into a wild whiteness. Turner and his contemporaries embellished such scenes with the wreckage of shipping hurled onto a rocky shoreline, but today's artists rarely witness such drama. Imbuing a sense of scale into such a scene is thus more difficult these days, especially when the storm is too wild even for the birds.

I remember one ferocious winter storm at Little Castle Point where the wind tore the pages of my sketchbook as I tried to make sense of the aerated water raging and roaring beneath me. Rendering detail of gigantic crashing waves, while exhilarating, does pose a challenge, especially when the paper is moving about of its own accord.

Rain complicates matters, but can be managed; wind is a different story, making a mockery of all attempts at joined-up sketching. By doing several sketches of the same scene hopefully some of the detail some of the time will be in the right place, and by amalgamating all the sketches a reasonably complete picture unfolds.

During the days of sail whenever a storm whipped up this coastline became transformed into a place of absolute terror for mariners. Over the years thousands of vessels perished in these waters. Before the coming of the railways most goods were moved by sea, so there was tremendous activity along the coast in the first half of the nineteenth

Wild Seas, Westdale Bay

*Earth-secrets, old, entombed, their stone enduring
the constant lash, the raking ebb and flow,
the cold green sucking tongues of waves exploring,
the rocks resist each punch the sea can throw.*

Jean M. Harvey

Marloes Beach   180 x 250mm

Marloes is a wonderful place for a picnic, walking, sketching, scrambling – or even playing cricket. Jenny relates her sporting dilemma:

Cricket brings out David's competitive side. When my two daughters, Joanne and Caroline, and David's daughter Catherine, join us for family holidays in Pembrokeshire at least one day on the beach is essential. Surrounded by four females, David is always confident he can beat us at beach cricket all by himself. So he is a one team and we four females are the other. So far he has yet to lose. We have tried everything: tying one arm behind his back, blindfolding him, insisting that he hops on one leg, but still the runs mount up, still the ball, like a guided missile, heads out to sea to the echo of his cackling while we run hither and thither. As soon as it is our turn to bat he bowls us out, one after another, with rarely a single run between us. On one occasion at Marloes we played well past sunset and were forced to admit defeat when the ball disappeared into the sea and the light was so bad we could not see to find it.

Wild Seas, Tower Point   300 x 470mm
Tower Point exudes a riveting presence from a number of angles
– see the sketch done from a different angle on page 64. When
the great sandstone battlements are being hammered by mighty
Atlantic waves, it is a compelling sight.

David Bellamy

Tower Point
This shows the far side of the view depicted in the painting on pages 62–63.

century. At times sixty or more ships might sail through the confines of Ramsey Sound on a single tide.

The Marloes-Dale Peninsula reaches out into the Atlantic, the coastline a fascinating mixture of hidden coves, beaches, high cliffs and shapely rock formations. Westdale Bay, with its jagged red sandstone rocks rising like anvils on the north side of the bay, is pictorially riveting at low tide when it affords greater potential for interesting compositions. Then one can scramble over rock ribs to view the southern part of the bay with Great Castle Head rising above.

To the north lies Marloes Beach, one of the gems of Pembrokeshire. Long may it remain undeveloped, for it boasts magnificent rock archi-

tecture. For the rock artist who likes a dip in the middle of a painting, this is paradise – well in summer, anyway. To the north-west the beach is bounded by Gateholm Island, and beyond this fascinating cliffs stretch all the way to Wooltack Point. My curiosity for these places knew no bounds: I just had to explore the lower cliff scenery between Marloes Beach and Renney Slip just over a mile away.

Because sketching would eat into the time, I needed three trips to cover the whole route, given the limitations caused by the tides, and as two of the trips included the family they tended to take longer, especially where everyone needs to rope down cliffs and ribs. Sometimes these traverses take hours just to cover a hundred yards or so, but they can be enormous fun.

Heavy Surf, Rickett's Head   250 x 390mm

So ferocious was the wind while I sketched that I had to lie flat out and weigh the book down with rocks. Even so, it took a tremendous buffeting, resulting in a rather animated, if tatty sketch. Coal was once mined on the cliff where I sketched, using bell pits and in later days 'slants' which led out under the sea. Behind me stood Trefane Cliff Colliery with its forlorn ruined chimney stack and other evidence of the old mine-workings. The coal was hauled to Nolton Haven in carts before loading onto vessels beached on the sand.

Storm at Renney Slip   380 x 610mm

The family resting during a coastal traverse: Catherine on the left, Jenny at the rear, Caroline sitting below her.

The middle section proved the most troublesome. I did this with Jenny in summertime, when shorts were the order of the day. Rarely is anything as easy as it looks from the cliff-tops, and much time was lost in roping down long stretches. We passed through Three Doors – three great gaps in a cliff which cuts off the next beach, with the outer 'door' already awash with the incoming tide. At the far end of the rocky beach a 30-foot/9m high rib of rock blocked further progress as it ran out into the sea.

I tried climbing a steeply-sloping chimney, but the rocks were so slippery that it was like trying to climb up the inside of a giant banana-skin. I retreated to the bottom. Elsewhere the rock mainly overhung, but then I jammed some stones into fissures in the greasy chimney and with some effort managed to scramble to the top. On the far side an easy-angled descent fell away, so I threw down the rope to Jenny and belayed her climb up to join me, doing the same down the far side.

Cave at Druidston

This sketch was carried out in wet weather using a watersoluble graphite pencil, and involved quite a bit of smudging to obtain a lovely soft effect.

Dinas Fach   180 x 310mm
This is a popular view seen from Newgale. The striking crags look for all the world like enormous pig's ears rising out of the sea.

Nolton Haven

I chose the wrong moment to do this watercolour sketch, as the sky remained dull until I finished. Then the sun came out and transformed the scene into a glorious one of amazing colour and light, the late afternoon sunshine bringing out the gorgeous warm variegated colours on the cliffs.

The author sitting on a cliff-top, sketching.

Solva   *210 x 310mm*

Solva is exceptionally popular with artists and visitors alike, whatever the season. John 'Warwick' Smith painted it in 1795, looking in the opposite direction to this view.

Ahead was an even higher rock rib, but we could just get round the seaward end before the tide cut us off. Losing no time, I leapt from rock to rock, judging each leap to coincide with the waves. Once across I turned to watch Jenny's progress. With a squeal she leapt across the boulders, but halfway across was caught by a large wave and totally saturated in the lower regions, dripping but in good heart as she scrambled onto the rock to join me.

At that point it was vital to check for an escape route, for our return would be cut off in minutes. Happily there appeared to be a route up the cliffs, and so we continued. At the far end of the beach progress was abruptly halted by the vertical cliff of Rainy Rock which ran well out to sea. We managed to climb a sloping slab to the side, then across a steep grassy slope to the top of the cliff.

By this time Jenny was fairly tired and did not want to continue, so I descended the 100 feet/30m or so on the far side and explored a bit more until the rising tide simply wouldn't allow any further effort. Not much had been done sketch-wise on this excursion, but it had been an interesting exercise, and it had sated my curiosity.

Off Wooltack Point lies Skomer Island, a birdwatcher's paradise whether you land on it or take a boat around the island. The National Park summer boat trips on a sunny evening combine stunning atmosphere, with the engrossing sight of thousands of birds, all furiously hurtling past. The puffins are particularly popular as their wings thrash furiously at some 400 beats per minute, whistling past the boat like comical Exocet missiles. Puffins, like rabbits, can be swallowed whole by black-backed gulls, which have an endearing habit of picking up rabbits, dropping them in the sea, and when suitably drowned, recovering and swallowing them.

Thousands of nesting birds cram along the cliffs, but perhaps one of the most arresting sights is that of a large string of Manx shearwaters coming in at dusk, all black and in perfect order. Suddenly, in unison they wheel to one side, turning over to reveal their white undersides as one. An amazing sight, repeated as they revert to their previous course.

Carn Rhosson from Porthlysgi

One of my favourite Pembrokeshire islands is Grassholm, for it had such an impact on all my senses when first I saw it, or rather, even before I saw it. Coming through the mist as we approached this most remote of the Pembrokeshire islands, I could smell the place before I could see it: 32,000 pairs of gannets leave their mark in more ways than one.

It appeared slowly out of the mist, at first an amorphous, ethereal shape glowing a brilliant white from the thousands of birds and their guano. As we came under the black cliffs on the north side of the island the air was alive with these large birds: looking up, especially with an open mouth, was ill-advised.

Strangely when my camera fell to bits on the way out and lay in my rucksack in several pieces it had happy, if rather expensive, consequences. This forced me to rely entirely on sketches without any photographic backup, and I was able to really concentrate on rendering the cliffs and birds, doing nine sketches as we worked our way slowly round the island which is slightly over quarter of a mile long.

Cavern, St Non's Bay   230 x 315mm

Seen here in serene evening light, the rock architecture on both sides of this cavern holds you spellbound as you canoe around it. Inside the swell rasped me up the side of the cavern several feet before dropping the canoe down again.

Shearwaters off Skomer

I used watercolour pencils, sketching from a bobbing boat to capture the image of these Manx shearwaters coming in at dusk, turning from black to white and back again as they wheeled to reveal their dark backs and white undersides, all in perfect unison. Sixty per cent of the world's population of shearwaters live on four of the Pembrokeshire islands.

Skomer

Shrieking gulls drown out the ghosts of Vikings –
these new invaders claimed and colonised
the island in their feathered tens of thousands
and now they rule the cliffs, the sea, the skies.

Seabird cities shudder at the onslaught,
battered by Atlantic gales and swell,
at Pigstone Bay the sea is never placid,
the Sounds' fast currents tug each sail and shell.

Man was here – the flints and ruins prove it –
his prehistoric sites, a trace of fields,
the rabbit-catchers and the patient farmers
dwindled with the land's decreasing yields.

The population now's all seals and puffins,
shearwaters outride wild weather's bluff.
Norsemen came and saw and then departed,
the birds stayed on – evolved from sterner stuff.

Jean M. Harvey

Vital Spark *off the Coast*   *220 x 330mm*

Creeling off Porthlysgi   320 x 480mm

Rising Tide, Porthclais   210 x 320mm

Back on the mainland coast, one of the most impressive features before reaching Little Haven is Tower Point, a huge red castellated rocky eminence that looks as though it has been sculpted out of the sandstone cliffs to form the airy stronghold of some demon king. It presents a magnificent spectacle from the south on the coast path, but it is worth leaving the path on the St Bride's side of it, to view it from the north-east at the edge of the cliffs.

Little Haven is a delightful jumble of cottages and shops, and for the artist generally best during the boating season, as these add considerably to its appeal. The artist can gainfully move boats around to hide unwanted features and add colour.

Further north along the coast stands the natural feature of Haroldston Bridge, not really visible from the coast path. Was it worth sketching? On closer inspection, a boat was clearly needed to properly sketch it

from the sea, but inland of the bridge lay a small cove surrounded on three sides by sheer cliffs. I decided to rope down into the cove.

At first all went well, but increasingly the cliff face became steeper, extremely loose and liable to collapse. Gingerly I continued downwards and came to a large rock on which I rested. At this point I created quite a bit of slack on the rope. As I moved down with one foot the large rock gave way. Down I crashed amid a deluge of rocks, stones, earth and a cloud of dust, bouncing down the face completely out of control, pencils flying in all directions. The rope tightened and brought me to a stop inches from the bottom, saving me from hitting the rocks and squashing my box of half-pans. I landed standing up in a rather strange stance, quite bemused.

After crossing to the far side of the cove I was able to sketch the rock bridge from under an overhanging part of the cliff. Lying around were a lot of new fallen rocks, some as big as a laundry basket. After a few

Twll y Gwyddel   220 x 280mm

Twll y Gwyddel – 'the Irishman's hole' – lies among the cluster of small islands at the southern end of Ramsey Island. In mist, the great rock pillar rising high above the water looks for all the world like some giant mythical beast about to devour the next boatload of tourists which dares to disturb its peace.

Gannets   240 x 175mm

moments sketching, a loud bang startled me out of my skin, and a rock crashed down from the cliff above. This was not comfortable terrain as I had no helmet, and a rather dynamic urgency was imbued in the pencil marks by one or two further crashes. I then climbed back up the cliff, a much easier task than the descent.

Nearby Druidston provides even more hideously life-threatening rock formations, should anyone be so foolish as to cross the portals of the shattered upper cliffs. The grimness of its dark coal measures are absurdly contrasted by the little seapinks flowering along these savage cliffs. At low tide the golden sands of Druidston Haven reveal an exciting mixture of cliffs, caves and rock.

Dinas Fach has also provided some interesting scrapes. On the west side is a huge cavern, visible from the top of the cliffs. I wondered whether it would yield a suitable picture, so one day abseiled into it with sketchbook accessible so that I could use it while on the rope, a useful method if you have to climb back up the rope using technical ascenders.

Alas, the composition did not merit a sketch, and my descent lay straight down into deep water, for which I was not kitted. I descended almost down to the rocks on the seaward side, then swung about. After a few pendulums I hit the far wall of the cave and thrust myself out with all my strength, sailing out over the rocks and releasing the descender as I did so, to crash-land on to the rib, from where I sketched something completely different.

Towards the end of a traverse on Dinas Fach, Jenny and I, clad in wetsuits, waded along the base of cliffs in deep, rising water, our rucksacks on our heads to protect the cameras, in the manner of the early explorers up the Limpopo. Not far off in a tiny cove, accessible only by boat, we could see a family, and a voice drifted over from them, 'There is only one person I know who would do something as daft as that – it must be David Bellamy!'

As we got closer I realised it was Mary Rees from Solva, who had joined us on a number of my painting courses. We chatted a while, then moved on, as Jenny could not swim and was concerned about the rising tide.

Grassholm – north cliffs   230 x 310mm

Where the island is covered liberally in gannet guano there is little colour on the north side of Grassholm, an image made more striking and sombre by the savage black cliffs. As I sketched I noticed one bird flapping feebly as it hung down the cliff, caught in a piece of fishing net which the gannets use to line their nests.

5
Crags and Cottages

Travelling northwards along the A40 towards Fishguard, the traveller soon reaches the Treffgarne Gorge, a great cleft with enormous rock buttresses riven by the Western Cleddau, beneath which stands Nant-y-Coy mill, a lovely old building which once had one of the most picturesque roofs in Pembrokeshire.

Like so many traditional old buildings, the new roof is functional but has taken away so much of the lovely old character of the place. The eastern side of the gorge is heavily-wooded while above the precipitous crags on the west, the moors rise to the arresting profiles of Maiden Castle and Poll Carn, Pre-Cambrian crags of resistant rhyolite which can be seen for miles.

Although this is not in the National Park, it is truly magnificent scenery. Under lowering skies and uncertain light on a grim day, the grotesque shapes in the rocks of Maiden Castle seem to dance like fiends from Hell. It is not difficult to conjure up images of the highwaymen who frequented the gorge in earlier times.

Treffgarne is said by some to be the birthplace of the great Welsh hero, Owain Glyndwr. From Great Treffgarne mountain northwards, the pleasant countryside undulates until west of Fishguard it rears up in a further flurry of craggy outposts on the Strumble Head peninsula, so characteristic of north Pembrokeshire.

Roch Castle from inland

Roch Castle   180 x 180mm

Pontiago cottages

The switchback spine bristles with crags, reminiscent of a line of sleeping dinosaurs. This makes a superb backdrop to scenes of farms and cottages, with their light-coloured roofs looking as though they've been smothered with custard. Trefasser holds several of these delights, though many need judicious re-arrangement of the topography to make them work as paintings. Textures, colour and shape come together in a glorious montage of vernacular delights in these humble dwellings.

The footpaths on this ridge on the Strumble Head peninsula vary in their friendliness: some begin as welcoming green swards, luring the unwary into a false sense of well-being but gradually deteriorating until one needs to hack a way forcefully through briars, gorse, wire and all manner of stout defences. It would be easier to retreat, but if you are nearing the end of a long circular walk, it is no fun to have to retrace one's steps. Anyway, my route is so often linked to a potential sketching subject, perhaps initially viewed through binoculars. If I am following a right of way to reach a better viewpoint, then the stroll can turn into an epic campaign – sometimes almost a siege – if the subject demands it.

On one occasion, coming down off the ridge and walking along a rough farm track with hedge-walls on either side, I suddenly realised a large horned beast was charging straight for me. Although I could not see it properly, it certainly seemed to have evil intent, and I was unsure whether the hedge-wall, low in places, would withstand a determined assault. So I leapt up on top of the hedge-wall opposite, ready to jump down into the far field and run, but quickly realised the animal was not a bull but a cow, and was slowing down and looking rather benignly at me. Perhaps she thought I had a bale of hay in my rucksack.

I continued along the lane and came to a farmyard gate behind which was a fierce-looking sheepdog, baring its teeth and barking at me. A few paces behind the sheepdog stood a huge Alsatian, growling and looking at me, clearly in anticipation of a good bite. Although the Alsatian was tethered, I could not see how far the chain extended. Should I climb on top of the wall and scout round the pair? No, I decided to take the sheepdog head-on and hope the Alsatian's chain was not too long.

Penbiri Hill from Dowrog Common   140 x 260mm

Seeking interesting new foregrounds to a familiar scene is part of the fun of being a landscape artist. I often tramp around a subject for hours searching in vain, including unlikely places such as Dowrog Common. Occasionally, these excursions throw up a gem like this old bridge.

walls a lovely shade of bright pink

Cottage near Treffgarne

Cottage near Treffgarne

Opposite: ***Carn Poll and Maiden Castle   290 x 220mm***
These impressive crags rise out of Treffgarne Mountain, and they are sketchable from numerous viewpoints.
For this winter sunset view I had to fight through thickets of thorn and briar, but it was well worth the effort.

Rhoddiad

This rough watercolour sketch I did as a quick demonstration for a painting course, to show the marvellous combination of colour washes and watercolour pencil lines. This fast technique is excellent for building up confidence.

Treffgarne Gorge and River Cleddau   210 x 295mm
This painting has been carried out on hand-made tinted paper of a blue-grey colour which imparts a strong hint of mood. The highlights have been brought out by white gouache, an opaque water-based paint which I sometimes use sparingly on ordinary white watercolour paper.

Carn Llidi and Carn Treliwyd

I held my rucksack down in front of my legs with my hands hidden from the dog, and pushed the gate open, striding straight at the sheepdog. He immediately took off in the opposite direction, but the Alsatian came straight at me. I moved slightly to one side and he quickly reached the end of his tether, so I was able to pass through the yard with some semblance of dignity.

One of my favourite parts of Pembrokeshire is the St David's peninsula, where rocky monadnocks (the remains of older once higher hills left by erosion) rise like high mountains, their lack of great height disguised by the sense of scale offered by the tiny dwellings which cling to their lower slopes and by the craggy nature of their upper parts. Penbiri Hill and Carn Llidi can easily be seen from Garn Fawr on Strumble Head on a clear day, with the Irish Sea beyond.

Ferocious winds sweep across this part of the countryside, evidenced by the many thorn trees sculpted into clipped shapes like stylised logos. There are no high trees here and in many places the ubiquitous Pembrokeshire hedgerows give way to stone walls. These hedge-walls are a delight to the artist, for they are constructed by laying a level of stones in the foundations, then a layer of soil, and continuing upwards with alternate stone and soil layers. Once this has matured, the soil layers sprout vegetation which not only binds the wall together but provides the artist with a ready-made 'lost and found' effect.

In any landscape painting, describing passages such as drystone walls can be repetitive and laborious, where it is easy to over-work matters by including every stone. The secret is to suggest a few stones and leave the rest to the viewer's imagination, but here with these hedge-walls a great

Rhosson Farm, St Justinian's   140 x 240mm
This farm, with its large round chimney and background crag which is often moved to right or left according to the artist's fancy, is a favourite with students on the St David's painting courses.

many of the stones are obliterated by hanging vegetation; the more haphazard, the better. As the hedge-walls are often topped with bushes and gorse, this adds to the pictorial attraction.

At Treleddyd Fawr stands a cluster of traditional cottages, a veritable gold-mine for the vernacular aficionado. These buildings boast a number of distinctive features which delight the landscape artist. Huge coarse porches often dominate the front aspect, with small windows recessed into rude stone walls. The kitchen chimney tends to be considerably larger than the one at the other end of the roof, but it is perhaps the roofs themselves that are the most outstanding feature.

The traditional method of roofing was a covering of slates reinforced by wires running from the roof ridge straight down to the eaves. Over all this would be laid a cement grouting, brushed on with a stiff house-brush, making the roofs light in tone, sometimes lighter than the walls. The grouting would seal the gaps between slates, many of which were rough. In bright sunshine it can be harsh on the eyes when sketching these structures, which gleam like beacons.

I have been sketching and painting here for many years, often with a group of students. On one occasion one student, a rather professorial type, took it upon himself to climb up on to the garden wall and stand there with his wife's frilly white hat stuck on his head, sketching the cottage. Given the right (or should it be wrong?) circumstances, even the most upstanding among us can become hooligans at times. Luckily nobody was at home.

The most picturesque and characterful cottage at Treleddyd Fawr is owned by Glyn Griffiths, who has stoutly maintained it in the traditional manner over the years. He is determined to continue doing so during his lifetime. Being a Grade II listed building, nothing much can be altered anyway. The walls, inside and out, are delightfully uneven. His companion is a large, affectionate cat named Ebrill, meaning April.

Strangely, although the Welsh Folk Museum at St Fagan's has a great many old Welsh buildings reconstructed there, they do not have one of these distinctive cottages – to my mind a dreadful omission. With a little imagination some of these lovely old buildings could provide an inspiring home to a museum of Pembrokeshire life.

St David's peninsula is criss-crossed with many footpaths, an ideal way of finding subjects to paint, and some of my painting courses are based on a walking theme. On one of these more active courses I took a group across Dowrog Common, making the classic mistake of checking the state of each end of the path beforehand, but not looking at the middle section because of a lack of time. This central part turned out to be exasperating. The path petered out, the ground became boggy and tussocky, and every time I looked round most of the students seemed to be upside down with their legs waving in the air. The only consolation was that this was an admirable place to fall over as the ground was rather soft… assisted by the rain which also created rather interesting effects on our watercolours.

St David's, of course, is the smallest city in Britain, the cathedral lying low in the valley of the River Alun where it would have been less conspicuous to Viking raiders. This river, according to Glyn Griffiths, was formerly known to the locals as Afon Duw, or God's River. Together with the Bishop's Palace, the cathedral makes a fine composition, but there are many fascinating corners to delight the wielder of a pencil.

Although the grand manner in architecture fascinates my eye, my pencil is drawn to the more humble buildings dotted about the landscape. In earlier times the abject poverty of the locals, when set against the vast wealth and opulence of the Bishop's Palace with its great halls, arcaded parapets and lavish stone carvings, would have been striking. The cathedral, originally constructed in the twelfth century, has been rebuilt many times, following Viking raids, vandalism and the attentions of Cromwell's troops. Much of the purple sandstone was quarried at nearby Caerbwdi Bay.

Opposite: *Carn Llidi*　*210 x 310mm*
Although only 595 feet/181m high, the crag presents a mountainous appearance, and is a handsome background to a variety of subjects, as well as often being the main feature. Quite often I find myself getting distracted by animals which can be curious when they see you sitting down in a field.

Dewi Sant, or St David, performed many miracles during his lifetime. One tale tells of how the Irish chieftain Boia, who dwelt on the nearby crag of Clegyr Boia, became infuriated when St David and his monks settled nearby to build the monastery, which would later become the site of the cathedral. Boia and his men set off to sort out this ecclesiastical upstart, but suddenly found themselves overcome by a strange fever. They retreated, only to find their cattle and sheep had all dropped dead. At this Boia returned to St David and asked for mercy, so David restored the animals to life and the two chaps became chums.

Alas, this was not good enough for the formidable wife of the Irish chieftain. She commanded her maids to go to where the monks could see them and frolic naked, use lewd words and play immodest games. The monks at this were sorely tried but St David remained firm and after a night of prayer by the following morning the chieftain's wife had become quite mad. The monks were no longer afflicted by the antics of the lewd maidens.

In 1990, the area was under threat from an Anglo-American plan to install 35 enormous radar aerials on the old airfield of St David's, which would have dominated the unique topography of the St David's peninsula for miles. All this slap-bang in the heart of a National Park, and with the attendant fears of health dangers caused by radiation. Prominent amid the resulting outcry against this potential devastation of the countryside was a group of artists who took the campaign to London. Happily this highlighted the threat, and backed by a well-organised campaign, forced the government to back off.

Roch Castle, a Peel tower at the western end of the Landsker, stands like a lone sentinel on a rhyolitic crag, surrounded by a cluster of buildings. It makes a fine composition from many angles, and is said to have been built by Adam de la Roche in the thirteenth century in order to defy a prophecy that he would die from the bite of a serpent. By accident or design we know not, but a viper was carried into the castle inside a bundle of firewood, and of course, poor old Adam inevitably died when he was bitten.

Fronhaul Cottage

St David's Cathedral   210 x 280mm

There are many delicious architectural treasures around the cathedral, and here I have brought a few of them together. Apart from the cathedral on the right, the left-hand monochrome depicts the grand entrance porch to the great hall of the Bishop's Palace. The combination of beautiful architecture and crumbling stone fascinated me. Above it I have painted the rose window of the Bishop's Palace, which is often at its best when caught in soft, mellow sunlight.

David Bellamy

Cottage at Treleddyd Fawr   210 x 280mm

*I have included Ebrill the cat in this scene, although I did not want to make her too conspicuous. In order to show more of the front of the cottage,
I have played down the wall a little.*

Frosty Morning *190 x 290mm*

We used to get many intensely cold, frosty mornings in Pembrokeshire when the windows of Penbank would be transformed into the most wondrous of fantastic frosted patterns. But these days it is rare to find a hard frost.

Overleaf: ***Farm below Garn Fawr***   ***280 x 460mm***

Pont Martin

Garn Fechan   200 x 300mm
This is the shapely spine that forms the backbone of the Strumble Head peninsula, like a line of sleeping dinosaurs.

Lane in late spring   125 x 250mm

So many Pembrokeshire lanes become a riot of colour in late spring when the wild flowers come into bloom. I especially love it when sunlight filters through the canopy of foliage to reveal highlights of these groups of flowers.

6
Preseli Moods

There is a wonderful sense of space and freedom and being away from it all when wandering along the Preseli ridges. Although only 1760 feet (536m), Foelcwmcerwyn, the highest Preseli summit can be viewed from most parts of Pembrokeshire.

Rarely do you meet many people up there, even at the height of the summer holidays, yet the walking is full of interest. As a youngster I would cycle up there to enjoy the wide open spaces of this spiritually uplifting place, where the very bones of the landscape seem to rise out of these gaunt hills.

Cottage below Carn Meini   190 x 230mm

Rhydwilym Chapel
I sketched this on a day when the Afon Cleddau roared past, completely submerging the road bridge, reminding me of the violent waters of the Urubamba River in Peru, only on a smaller scale.

7

Mischief on the North Coast

From St David's Head north-eastwards to Poppit Sands, where Pembrokeshire joins Ceredigion, the coastline continues its wild contortions, embracing some of the most savage rock scenery in Wales.

The brooding cliffs are only briefly punctuated by harbours in few places, but here and there these stern ramparts are broken up by some of the most attractive beaches in Pembrokeshire. In places, the wild countenance of this north coast is further accentuated by the high rocky summits running down to the coastline.

Cormorants

Cottages at Abereiddi

The old roofs were more picturesque,
poignant in their disrepair,
their grouted curves like prows of ships
gnawed away by salt-sharp air.

They've been replaced now – modernised
and though immune to draft and leak,
they've traded in all character
and lost what made them so unique.

The modern builder seems at odds
with artisans of rustic style,
his soulless efforts seldom spark
an interested gaze or smile.

True restoration's art requires
a hand that does more good than harm –
aesthetics rule, so tell us, do –
just when it was they outlawed charm.

Jean M. Harvey

Abereiddi   170 x 200mm
I have painted these cottages as they were a few years ago, with their mouth-wateringly delicious roofs.

Torn by continual winds, St David's Head, the north-west cornerstone of the county, often presents a bleak prospect to coast-walkers. The countless indentations on the north side give one a constant sense of being on the verge of discovering some exciting hidden cove, perhaps where pirates are unloading contraband.

I love to combine this part of the coast with a scramble up craggy Carn Llidi. The route can be varied, but the view from the summit is always rewarding. Sea mists often create strange effects on the crag, and it has provided many compositions over the years. In his 1795 painting of St David's Head, Turner made his boatmen the size of ants to emphasise the wild topography.

Continuing up the coast, we pass beneath the heights of Penbiri Hill, another crag with splendid views from the top, accessible from the coastal side. From the top of the cliffs, the prospect of a savage coastline culminating in Strumble Head stretches ahead for miles. At Castell Goch, an Iron Age fort, a jagged wall of serrated slate thrusts out over Porth Tre-wen. The shattered castle-like promontory appears as a fitting lair for some ferocious sea-demon. You might well shudder as you sneak quietly past, relieved when Abereiddi heaves into view.

The only facilities at Abereiddi are toilets and in summer an ice-cream van. This is an excellent place to take groups of painters, for there is plenty of room to spread out to paint a host of subjects, from the many picturesque cottages, the bay and the cliffs with their fascinating textures and colours. When artist Rod Williams ran his popular courses in St David's, he would sometimes bring his group to Abereiddi when my course was also there.

I remember on one occasion there must have been at least 25 artists scattered around the place and I passed by one of my students all afternoon, giving her a smile but no tuition, as I thought she was one of Rod's. It was after all our first day, and she had changed her top, put on a large hat and made herself look totally different.

The cottages over the years have themselves been ravaged by storms, one of which completely wrecked a row of old workers' cottages. As so often on the Pembrokeshire coast, late spring is a lovely time here when wild flowers add to the scene, like some wild over-run garden around the shapely buildings.

Stack at Carregwastad Point
Said to be the haunt of mermaids, but I've not seen many here.

Penrhyn cottage and cliff

Penrhyn Cottage

What keeps it there? What claw, invisible,
clamped to the cliff-top's rim can anchor safe
this shell of whitewashed stone?
It hugs the ground as though
its sloping roof and pale squat chimneys know
the sun's warm light is doomed to fade.
And they prepare – walls tense,
the black unwinking windows stare,
wait for the cold, the next determined storm.

Jean M. Harvey

Penbiri and Carn Llidi from Trefin

St David's Head from the north-east *120 x 250mm*
This view is from Pwllderi – a marvellous place to watch sunsets – and shows Penbiri Hill and Carn Llidi rising above the coastline.

Overleaf: ***Porth Glastwr*** *310 x 500mm*
This is a savage place at the best of times. The bay probably gets its name from the prominent green tower, which acts as the focal point here.

Beyond the hamlet lies the Blue Lagoon, a man-made gash in the cliffs, popular with cliff-jumpers who provide interest should one get bored painting. Jumping off cliffs is unlikely to catch on in a big way. It involves leaping off rocks at ever-increasing heights, going as high as you dare, and preferably aiming to hit the water on the way down. Some of the students also scramble around looking for subjects, and as a consequence I have occasionally lost one or two temporarily, or had to risk getting a wetting in traversing to give them tuition.

From here it is only a short stretch to Porthgain, a small harbour over-looked by the massive brick storage hoppers which once held the crushed and graded stone before it was loaded on to sailing vessels moored in the harbour. The industrial bustle and activity of the late nineteenth century declined at the onset of the First World War, but Porthgain still has relics of those days which evoke an atmosphere that is different from any other Pembrokeshire coastal village. The artist really has to look hard to find the true spirit of the place; but it is there to those who spend time contemplating the scene.

Aberdraw, the cove west of Trefin, overlooked by its ruined mill, has shapely rocks and cliffs, and a natural arch through which one can view a summer sunset – preferably with the tide out. It was here we filmed for a video on painting coastal scenery, and I was encouraged to move out further on the rocks than I thought wise, in order that I could be seen against a glorious sunset.

The inevitable happened: as I became engrossed in the sketch a massive wave knocked me over. I had some difficulty hanging on to both rocks and sketchbook, with my hearing completely knocked out for a while, and with it my sense of balance. I managed to scramble back onto the rock – without looking at the camera, as I assumed all was being filmed.

Once back in position, I continued sketching, but ready for another dousing. Alas, the next wave was even bigger and hammered me across the rocks like a spider being washed down a plug-hole. Completely immersed, I simply hung on as best I could, feeling as though I'd just been through the rinse and spin cycle of a washing machine. Eventually

I scrambled back up and this time looked round to ensure they were still filming. The crew had actually packed up, and were about to set off for the pub! Unfortunately, they had missed the second dousing.

West of Pwllstrodur lies some of the most visually terrifying of Pembrokeshire coastal scenery, monstrous anvils rearing out of the water beneath vertiginous cliffs like some Herculean smithy, a scene of the most grim awesomeness when wreathed in mists and crashing seas. These anvils are not easy to sketch, as you either have to rope down to obtain a better perspective, or use a boat beneath the intimidating cliffs. It is wise to ensure the sketchbook is firmly attached when sketching on the end of a rope above a churning sea.

We now stray into the area which in 1797 witnessed the last invasion of Britain, an episode that ranged from the tragic to the farcical. When four French ships arrived off Fishguard on 22 February, the locals had been aware of them for some time. Unfortunately the Fishguard defences had only one cannon-ball with which to sort out the enemy vessels, which did not auger well. However, the moment the fort opened up with this tremendous broadside, the French fleet fled. Not to be outdone, they waited round the corner until after dark and then ferried their troops ashore by moonlight at Carregwastad Point, up awkward, shelving and steep rocks.

The French objective was to spread unrest. They set up headquarters at Trehowel Farm under their commander, an American named Colonel Tate, who curiously could not speak French. Their ships returned to France. Foraging parties looted the local farms which were awash with wine recovered from a Portuguese vessel which had recently foundered on the coast. As a consequence, many Frenchmen became rather drunk.

Several scraps took place between the local farmers and the invaders, including the arrest of a dozen Frenchmen by Jemima Nicholas, a formi-dable local cobbler lady who set about the French with a pitchfork before single-handedly surrounding them and escorting them to Fishguard jail. At Bristgarn Farm there still stands a grandfather clock with a French bullet-hole through it, caused by some jumpy invader.

Misty morning, Abercastle   210 x 260mm

Like many small coastal villages around Wales, Abercastle grew out of coastal trading, until the coming of roads and lorries made it redundant. Often, to make every minute count while the tide was right, the horses and carts would actually go alongside the ship with their lower parts awash.

Sketch from belly-boat – Cwm-yr-eglwys
This was a sketch done in such exquisite comfort that I almost fell asleep while drawing, lulled by the lapping water and balmy morning sunshine. It shows the evocative remains of St Brynach's church.

Opposite: **Old Harbour, Fishguard**   *230 x 205mm*
The old harbour area boasts many fascinating compositions for the artist, and every time I visit there seems to be something new to paint.

The Needle near Fishguard   310 x 480mm

I first sketched this feature from the top of the cliffs, a rather challenging aspect from the acute perspective, but this view was originally sketched from a fishing boat, with the skipper gallantly trying to maintain position for about twenty minutes or so.

A dramatic rescue

In December 1920, this was the scene of a dramatic rescue, when the Dutch motor schooner Hermina *dragged her anchors for some considerable distance in the teeth of a storm. Darkness had fallen when the Fishguard lifeboat* Charterhouse *was alerted by distress flares from the stricken vessel. Coxswain John Howells anchored the lifeboat to windward of the vessel, and at tremendous risk managed to get ropes across. The raging sea threw the lifeboat into the schooner's rigging, yet despite this terrifying prospect the lifeboatmen got seven Dutchmen off the ship. However, Captain Vooitgedacht and his chief officer and second mate refused to leave the ship, even though Coxswain Howells indicated that it would be impossible to return. They still refused.*

By now the lifeboat, having taken tremendous punishment, was leaking and the engine failed to start. Under the sheer cliffs, the prospect looked grim. When the lifeboatmen raised the mizzen sail in an attempt to sail the boat out of danger, the ferocious wind tore the sail to ribbons, leaving only the mainsail. Two men then managed to crawl forward and set the jib sail while waves continually crashed over them. By superb seamanship, the lifeboat crawled away from the threatening cliffs under sail and oars, and about three hours later made Fishguard Harbour.

Again maroons went up from the schooner as the vessel began to founder on the rocks. By now rocket apparatus had been erected on the cliffs. The Dutch captain and chief officer managed to cross onto the rocks and were hauled to safety, but the second mate drowned. Coxswain Howells was awarded the RNLI Gold Medal and three of the crew received silver medals.

Meanwhile, Lord Cawdor on hearing the news marched his Castlemartin Yeomanry up to North Pembrokeshire and gathered together all the local volunteers. This amounted to under 600 in number, to counter the 1400 or so in the French force.

Whether by accident or design, the defenders were reinforced by hundreds of Welsh women in their black hats and scarlet cloaks, apparently with stakes, pitchforks, pokers and all manner of improvised weapons. From a distance they appeared like an endless force of British grenadiers as they wound round a nearby hill. The French on seeing this force promptly gave up, and the surrender was signed in the Royal Oak Inn.

In 1997, a French contingent came over and the event was re-enacted. A tapestry, now shown in Fishguard town hall relates the story of the invasion. As for Jemima the heroine, you can spot her around the town these days, often complete with pitchfork, in the form of Yvonne Fox, who took the part of Jemima in the re-enactment and has worked wonders for local tourism.

The old harbour at Fishguard is a great favourite among artists and photographers, its picturesque cottages straddling the road along the top of the harbour wall. I adore the texture and puddles at low tide, criss-crossed by chains and ropes and the rusty old hulls of the fishing boats. Every visit yields different material, with boatmen mending boats, nets or whatever. By getting down into the harbour, each watery channel, rope, chain or length of seaweed tells its own exciting tale. Even dollops of mud can have an aesthetic purpose when employed judiciously in a scene.

Dinas Island to the east of Fishguard is a prominent landmark. At the western end of the valley which connects it to the mainland, for it is not a real island, lies Pwllgwaelod, a beach with high cliffs on its southern flank. The old Sailor's Inn has the air of a smugglers' retreat, a popular place especially in summer, when the garden is often filled with walkers.

At low tide the bottom of the cliffs affords an interesting traverse route, initially along a narrow ledge, scrambling up and down ridges often

David and Jenny about to go canoeing: note the waterproof map case to contain sketch-paper, in Jenny's hand.

Opposite: ***Cottage at Cwm-yr-eglwys   260 x 210mm***
For such a tiny place, Cwm-yr-eglwys has a rich array of paintable nooks and crannies. I loved the way the stream tumbled down the rocky water-course onto the beach.

David Bellamy

Cat Rock and Parrog
So often, a few simple strokes are all that is needed to make an effective composition.

Parrog, Newport **180 x 240mm**

Parrog is another of my favourites, moving boats around to suit the mood of the day with backgrounds that range from extremely simple to quite complicated buildings.

sharp, slippery and splashed by waves as you try to progress, unsure how far you can get. Pebble beaches end in more rock-scrambling, then comes a through cave with greasy rocks covered in vivid green weed. Should I be going back? How often have I been caught by the tide and had to jump in and wade to safety after getting lost in a sketch?

Eventually the route runs into deep water. There is no going any further without some flotation device. I retreat a few yards and then climb up a slidey-shaley gully, steep and uncompromising. One step up, two down. Below me a seal pops its head above the water and laughs mockingly at me. I reach the top of the cliffs and take only a few minutes to return to Pwllgwaelod, when the outer traverse has taken me hours, with all the sketching and scrambling.

At the eastern end of the valley from Pwllgwaelod lies Cwm-yr-eglwys, 'the valley of the church'. The church itself, St Brynach's, was like many buildings on this coast, destroyed in a storm in 1859, and all that remains is one end and the bell-tower, a graphic memorial to the forces of nature. There is much to interest the artist here, without the need to resort to traversing or getting wet in any way. I did, however, use my bright red belly-boat on one occasion to explore cliff scenery to the east.

Launching early into the bay, there were few around to witness the event. I left Jenny sketching and Catherine reading on the beach and silently flipped my way round the headland to work on a series of sketches, some from rocks onto which I landed, and some from the belly-boat itself. Occasionally a small fishing boat would appear and on catching sight of me would come to within about 100 yards (90m) to investigate, a problem most artists encounter, one way or another. As they discreetly looked in my direction I gave them a wave and they would then happily go away.

Eventually I floated back into the bay of Cwm-yr-eglwys, enjoying the wonderful sense of freedom. Sketching from the belly-boat is one of the most relaxing pastimes I've experienced. By this time many folk had arrived on the beach and rocks and it was noticeable that their conversation stopped dead as I floated past reading a copy of *The Times*, with no visible means of propulsion. How I wished I'd been wearing a bowler hat! Looking around I could see Jenny and Catherine wondering whether to help me out or pretend not to know me. Jenny carried on sketching, trying to ignore my approach – but Cath did render some assistance – in between laughs. I flopped on the beach feeling fully invigorated.

The coast from here to Newport has much to delight the artist, photographer – and belly-boater. In summer, Parrog, the port area of Newport, is resplendent with boats scattered about, making it easy to find one with a picturesque backdrop such as Cat Rock, Dinas Head or many of the old buildings along the front. It is especially lovely in the evening. Inland the town rises up towards the castle and above to the shapely summit of Carn Ingli, the northernmost tip of the Preseli range.

This is the estuary of the Afon Nyfer, or River Nevern, another favourite, for on either side of the estuary the artist can paint numerous scenes, whatever state of the tide or weather. I rather enjoy it when rain squalls sweep across Newport Bay, losing all the detail and providing an exciting atmosphere as a backdrop to boats, buildings or whatever is my centre of interest.

Opposite: **Boat at Sunset and Dinas Head   220 x 320mm**
Another painting done on tinted paper, this time the biscuit-coloured de Wint paper, thin and lumpy but sadly no longer made. Even when stretched it cockles violently and is at times like painting on the back of a pustuled toad.

Wind-sculpted trees   90 x 100mm

These trees feature in many of my north Pembrokeshire paintings, and several students who were familiar with my work were surprised when visiting the county for the first time, they saw these trees. They had assumed I had made up such weird shapes.

Nyfer Estuary in mist   210 x 340mm
On both banks of the Nyfer Estuary stand a wealth of varied compositions, but so often it pays to be selective in choosing the limits of the work. In this rendering, mist provides a way of concentrating on the cottage as a focal point.

A Final Word

The natural beauty and tranquillity of *Gwlad hud a lledrith* has been extolled by many down the years. In today's violent world such places provide an opportunity for quiet contemplation, relaxation and spiritual antidote, but this rural idyll is fragile.

For centuries Pembrokeshire folk have had a great tradition for independence and in speaking their minds against injustice and the imposition of destructive influences by external agencies. In recent years they have rejected many potentially damaging proposals, such as that of nuclear storage at the former Trecwn naval depot; the Anglo-American radar installation at St David's airfield; the plan to burn Orimulsion at Pembroke Dock; and the attempt to introduce GM crops into North Pembrokeshire, which attracted a latter-day appearance of Rebecca and her daughters.

The underhand methods of many in authority, from the highest in the land, downwards, become revealed in stark relief at times, graphically illustrated by their cavalier attitude to the *Sea Empress* disaster of 1996 and its aftermath. Whatever colour the spin doctors, they all seem to have the same aim – to bleed the locals in order to feather corporate nests and advance their own debased ends.

It is small businesses, run by indigenous folk and incomers alike that keep Wales running, not the conglomerates that are threatening to tear up Cardigan Bay in pursuit of oil, or the appalling march of massed wind-farms across the Welsh landscape, industrialising our finest natural scenery. Both these threats, which mainly benefit foreign interests, could severely damage this outstanding landscape and, as a consequence, the Pembrokeshire economy. Wind turbines in particular cost the taxpayer millions in subsidies, produce a pathetic amount of energy and need 100 per cent continuous back-up from power stations.

All those who love the Welsh countryside would do well to remain alert to these devious and at times sinister intrusions into our few remaining areas of natural landscape. The wildscapes of Pembrokeshire must be preserved for our children so that they may remain in touch with the real earth, and enjoy nature at its most magnificent, for this is truly a very precious and magical landscape, perhaps best summed up by the words of Lord Byron:

> *There is a pleasure in the pathless woods,*
> *There is a rapture on the lonely shore,*
> *There is society, where none intrudes,*
> *By the deep sea and music in its roar*

Acknowledgements
I should like to express my thanks to Jenny Keal for checking the manuscript and helping to piece it all together; to Jean M. Harvey, formerly Jean M. Thomas, who has produced such marvellous poetry to complement the artwork; to Roly Smith for editing my challenging copy; Glyn Griffiths for his local knowledge.